# SOPHIE
## goes to Death Valley

Written by Tammy Pounds
Illustrated by Katie Merrill

# Hi, I'm Sophie!

You may know me as Sophie the Super Host from my home at Casa Blanca, in Ridgecrest, California. When I'm not being a super host with Airbnb, my person and I like to go exploring. Some of my favorite places to visit are National Parks.

Today, I'm visiting Death Valley National Park.

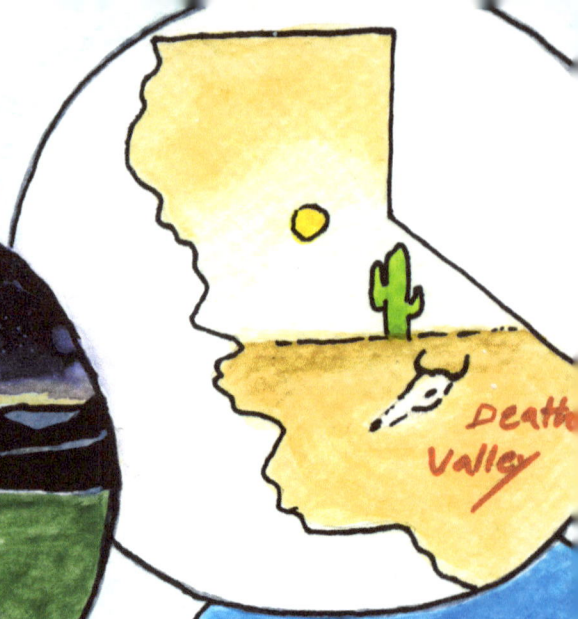

Death Valley

Let me tell you why Death Valley Is so special. It Is the largest national park with over 3.4 million acres. Visitors to the park average over a million people a year. It's In two states, California and Nevada.

It's one of only a few International Dark Sky Parks, so It's the perfect place for stargazing.

Death Valley Is a geological wonderland! There are an array of wild animals and plants if you look closely.

If you are lucky, you may see Death Valley come to life with a Super Bloom. It's a beautiful show of flowers that cover the landscape In shades of gold, white and purple.

The drive takes about an hour and a half from where I live, and there Is lots to see along the way.

Come along with me and let's get ready to go.

We will need water, extra If It's summer, a hat, and a jacket or long sleeve shirt. You need to plan for all temperatures. It Is the land of extremes. Death Valley Is the hottest place on earth! It reached a high temperature of 134.1 degrees Fahrenheit or 56.7 Celsius, and Is a true desert, warm to hot In the day, but once the sun goes down It can really cool off.

Last, but not least, a full tank of gas, and check that you have a spare tire and that it's aired up, and the tools to change it, just in case. Also, you will have little, if any, cell phone reception most of the day, so download your maps so they work offline or have a paper map.
Now, Let's go!!

If you like horses, bring carrots or apples and stop at the Ridgecrest Regional Wild Horse and Burro Corrals. Did you know that a Burro and a Donkey are the same? Their scientific name is Equus Asinus. They have a dark stripe down their backs and part way down their front legs. They are rounded up from the desert to keep them healthy. Then people can adopt them.

Back on the road.
Next, we come to the Trona Pinnacles. Seeing the Pinnacles from the road they look small in the distance. It's a unique and amazing geological formation. The spires, called Tufas, once rose from the bottom of an ancient lakebed. Some are small like coral, and others are over 140 feet tall. Scientists think they could have been covered by 640 feet of water and that this water was one of a chain of lakes and rivers leading to Death Valley.

Speaking of Death Valley-let's get back on the road! While you're In the car keep a look out for the Fish Rocks! The rocks were painted between the 1930's and 1940's. However, In the 1970's a group painted them back to "rock" color. Not long after they were re-painted to the way you see them today. The road used to run right by the rocks but would sometimes get washed out when It rained so the road was moved.

Do you know the game I Spy?
On your Drive look out for wild
burros and horses roaming
around.
Also, coyotes, rabbits, snakes
and lizards

One of my favorite spots in Death Valley is a place called Darwin Falls.
The spring-fed water comes down the canyon and splits into an upside-down Y when it meets a rock. It's a beautiful year-round waterfall.

There is sometimes a pond but not always. I have seen it both ways.

It's usually an easy 30-minute walk from the trailhead with a little bouldering closer to the falls.
However, there was a big storm in 2023 that washed away the road to the trailhead, so for now, it's about a 9 mile round trip hike. If you make it all the way, you've really earned it. There are also upper falls, but the trail is not marked.

Do you like art?
If so, you'll love our next stop, Mosaic Canyon. This place is known for its beautiful mosaic-like rock patterns that make this area a geologic art gallery. You will also walk through some amazing slot canyons.

While there are multiple spots for sand dunes, the most well-known is the Mesquite Sand Dunes.

You will see several types of sand dunes here. There are crescent, linear and star shaped dunes.

Dunes are formed when years of wind erode the mountains into sand, and that sand, gets trapped by bushes and trees and piles up creating dunes.

The biggest dune at Mesquite
is 100 feet tall.

Park your car and slide down
the dunes.

You'll have sand in your
pockets, shoes and hair.

Once you're done having fun
here, shake yourself off and
get back in the car and head
to Zabriskie Point.

The Badlands at Zabriskie Point are dramatic.
They were created when rain washed fine silt and volcanic ash down to an ancient lake and made clay and sandstone.
I love how the sunlight casts shadows on the hills making Zabriskie look different depending on what time of day you see it.
Recommended as a sunrise viewing spot.

Artist Palette Drive is gorgeous and unique.

The drive is a loop that will take you through canyons where you can explore the colorful mountains.

The vivid colors of red, orange, yellow, blue, purple, pink and green, are made from volcanic deposits of minerals that have oxidized. The rainbow effect is created by iron oxides, copper, mica, manganese, and chlorite, to name a few.

Dante's View showcases the valley from over 5,000 feet above the valley floor and offers a stunning panoramic view.
You can see the Badwater Basin, which is well below sea level.
This is a popular vantage point to see the vastness of the park. I love to see the sunset from here.
The sky often shows an array of beautiful shades of pinks, oranges, purples and blues.
On to the lowest point in the Continental
United States!

BADWATER BASIN
282 FEET/855 METERS

BELOW SEA LEVEL

Badwater Basin is almost 300 feet below sea level. Because it is the lowest point, there is a high concentration of Sodium, Calcium and Magnesium minerals. It was an ancient lake that evaporated leaving behind a visible layer of salt. Depending on the season there may or may not be water here. When there is water, it's 4x saltier than the ocean.

While it might be tempting to walk out to the water, stay on the boardwalk so as not to crush the tiny Badwater Snails. They live under the salts crust and feed on algae.

Within the park are several craters.
The largest is called Ubehebe Crater,
which is
600 feet deep and 1/2 mile across.
Not far from here is little Ube.
Little Ube is the youngest.
Scientists believe it was formed about 2,100 years ago.
You will notice many, many dark purple rocks in varying sizes.
These make up what are called the cinder fields.

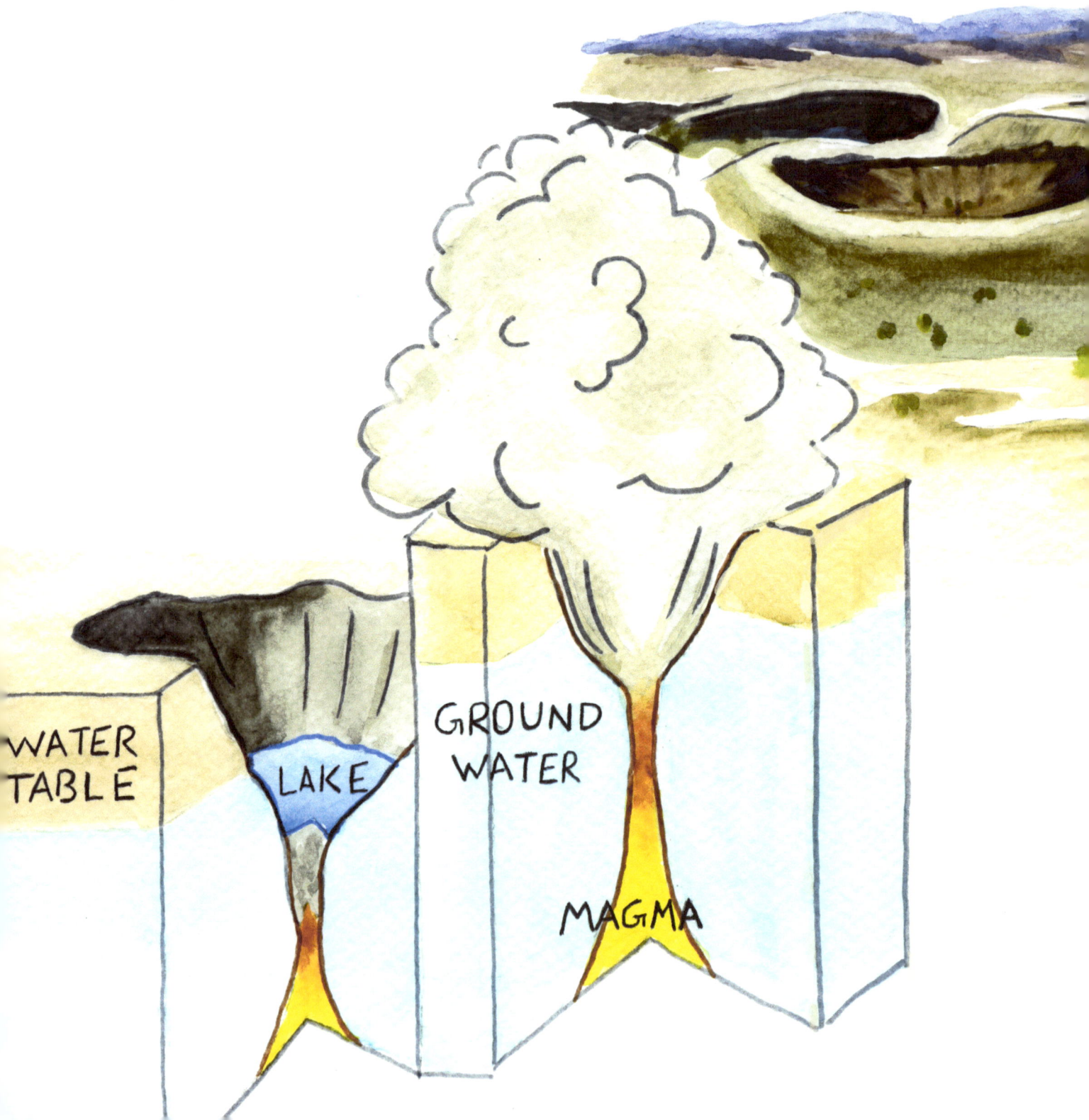

WATER
TABLE

LAKE

GROUND
WATER

MAGMA

These craters were formed
from steam and gas
explosions.
When magma from deep In
the earth rose up and
encountered groundwater.
These are called Marr
Volcanos.

You can explore the crater, but a
few words of caution: getting
down
is easier than getting back up,
even if you're in good shape like
me.
You can walk around the rim or
just take it
in from the viewpoint.
Rocks are sharp.
Always
use caution.
As for me,
I like to imagine the explosion
that made such
a big crater.

Within Death Valley is a magical place named Scotty's Castle.
It is closed to the public for tours after floods and a fire but is worth mentioning.
A two-story Mediterranean masterpiece that was a luxury estate for the time.
It had several natural springs that allowed it to flourish in the desert heat.

Millionaires Albert and Bessie Johnson came to Death Valley with the hopes of attaining more riches in gold, but they quickly fell in love with the beauty of the land. The Castle is named after their friend and partner, "Death Valley Scotty," who lured them there with the promise of gold, in the 1920's.

Have you ever eaten a date before?

A date is a delicious treat, and I love treats!
It tastes like candy and is full of fiber and very nutritious.
It has many minerals and has superfood properties.
Death Valley has a date farm called the China Date Farm. It's a neat place to learn about different varieties and why the desert is the perfect place for them to grow.
Other places where dates grow are Arizona, California, Iran, Saudi Arabia, and Egypt.

I love learning! Did you know that even though Death Valley is one of the driest places on earth it has a wetland and is full of life? Ash Meadows National Wildlife Refuge is an International Ramsar site. It was among the first and the largest in the United States. What is that you might ask? Well, it is a Wetland of international importance and is protected.

Ash Meadows has at least 26 endemic species, meaning they are only found here!
It has the largest concentration of endemic species In the United States.
As the last Oasis In the desert, It's a rare and unique eco-system that Is thriving and plays an important roll In global conservation and education.
It Is home to many endangered species Including the Pup Fish named for the way they look while they are swimming resembling puppies at play.

There are plants and animals that can only be found In Death Valley  and nowhere else In the world.
That Is what endemic means. You may see birds, lizards, bobcats or bighorn sheep. While there are many other spots In Death Valley National Park to discover, this gives you a place to start.

We hope you love Death Valley as much as we do! Be mindful, enjoy the beauty of this magnificent place but leave no trace. Explore our big, beautiful world.
Be curious and kind.
See you In my next adventure,

Sophie

**Tammy Pounds** grew up at the base of the Sierra Nevada mountains in the community of Ridgecrest, California. Where the people look out for one another, making it the perfect place to raise four children. She loves National Parks and is fortunate to be driving distance to many. She is thankful for the forethought to preserve these places of natural beauty so they can be enjoyed for future generations. She credits her grandfather as her inspiration to be a writer and active in the community. When she's not exploring, you will likely find her writing, in the kitchen cooking or baking, teaching yoga, bee keeping, or playing with her dog Sophie who is the real-life character in her books.

**Sophie** has been a member of the family since she was a puppy. She Is 10 years old. Sophie loves to play, go on walks, and especially loves her people and is the kindest, most lovable dog. You can usually find her carrying around one of many toys. They often enjoy a sunrise or sunset together.

**Katie Merrill** is a young artist, currently living in her childhood town of Ridgecrest California. She loves to eat ice cream, go camping, and watch romcoms! Ever since she was little, she wanted to be a professional artist, and now that dream is actually coming true. She hopes to eventually illustrate more stories and spread her creativity!

www.ingramcontent.com/pod-product-compliance
Lightning Source LLC
Chambersburg PA
CBHW060822270326
41931CB00002B/58